WINDSWEPT

poems and photos by Michelle Terry

Copyright © 2021 by Michelle Terry. All rights reserved.

This book or any portion thereof may not be reproduced or used in any manner whatsoever without the express written permission of the publisher except for the use of brief quotations in a scholarly work or book review. For permissions or further information contact Braughler Books LLC at:

    info@braughlerbooks.com

Page 42-43 photo © Cody James Tracy

Printed in the United States of America
Published by Braughler Books LLC., Springboro, Ohio

First printing, 2021

ISBN: 978-1-970063-95-0 soft cover
ISBN: 978-1-955791-18-2 hard cover

Library of Congress Control Number: 2021905959

Ordering information: Special discounts are available on quantity purchases by bookstores, corporations, associations, and others. For details, contact the publisher at:

    sales@braughlerbooks.com
    or at 937-58-BOOKS

For questions or comments about this book, please write to:

    info@braughlerbooks.com

With love to Jo March and anybody else who didn't think they could.

Contents

Poetry ... 6

Pretty Little Words ... 9

Woodsmoke Silence ... 10

Calibration ... 13

Sitting in Sonder ... 14

Patina ... 17

What Do the Trees Say ... 18

Ritual ... 21

Today, I Sit Grateful ... 22

Carpe Diem ... 25

In Pursuit of Goldilocks ... 26

Lessons in Barbed Wire ... 29

Soft Sadness ... 30

Flipped Switch Float Trip ... 33

Learning How to Sleep Again ... 34

A River Runs Through Me ... 37

Sleeping in an Astral Bed ... 38

Windswept ... 41

Forest Bath ... 43

Tomatoes ... 44

Liminal Autumn ... 47

Autumnal Equinox - A Venerable Checklist ... 48

Solstice March (in December) ... 51

Reconnection ... 52

Sunflower ... 55

Moon in Passing ... 56

Hanging Curve Ball of Space ... 59

In the Pecan Orchard ... 60

Unsupervised ... 63

Sinusoidal Curves ... 64

Scent of Soon It'll be Autumn ... 67

Following the Azimuth ... 68

Lay my Limbs ... 71

The View ... 72

Poetry

You don't have to understand it to feel it.

Your head shouldn't hurt when you read it.

Windswept takes you on a photographic journey through the riverbeds, caverns, and starscapes of your heart.

Roll down the windows and enjoy the ride.

Pretty Little Words

Sometimes, words are petals
An utterance of play and nonsense
A habit to fill uncomfortable silence
Build houses of cards and share recipes
IKEA directions and crochet patterns

My words live on paper, in notebooks
On blinking screens and seed packets
Phrases of threes and fives
Prolific. Yes. Epic? No way.
But these words are mine
Cherished
Revered
Silent
Gulped and swallowed inside my throat
Pressed down until they surface as enigmas
buried inside veiled poetry, garden plots, and ovens

During the best of times, the words are ours
Passed between each other in the mason jar
Secrets we have not even told to ourselves
Our thoughts dancing among the fireflies
Never quite touching, never quite letting go
Yearning to speak what lies below

Woodsmoke Silence

I sit silent by the fire and sip
Soak in September's woodsmoke
Listen to the lilt of conversation
Leap from mouth to mouth
I have reached an age
where I exercise the right
to sit quiet without remorse
Though, interested and engaged
No longer have I the urge
to speak my opinions out loud
I will save my hoarded words for
only those battles I need to wage

Calibration

If nowhere is a place
then I'm in the middle of it
On a two-lane
Where pastel-kissed sky
hugs the prairie
Antelope mamas and babes
graze easy next to the cattle

With each rural route curve
I feel myself calibrate
My heart clicks to the tick
where I am most content
Chronically flighty feet
finally anchor to the ground
and I breathe

Finding peace inside spiral
Comfort within the
spaces in between
My soul grateful for
being exactly where I am

Sitting in Sonder

Today, I say good morning!
To you, the heron and the owl
I inhale the earth's daybreak
Exhale remnants of the day before
Pinks and oranges and blues
Creamsicle kaleidoscope backdrop
to dots of bluejays and crows sending
their raucous hellos as they fly overhead

I can't find the words today
they are a delicate ether swimming
inside, in and around, and all over
Two fishes in the Tropic of Cancer
One with the tide, the other against
I know I'm not alone in this trek
The ebb and flow of our days
So, to you I say good morning
I feel your life, your love, your intricacies
Even through life's smoky, somnolent haze

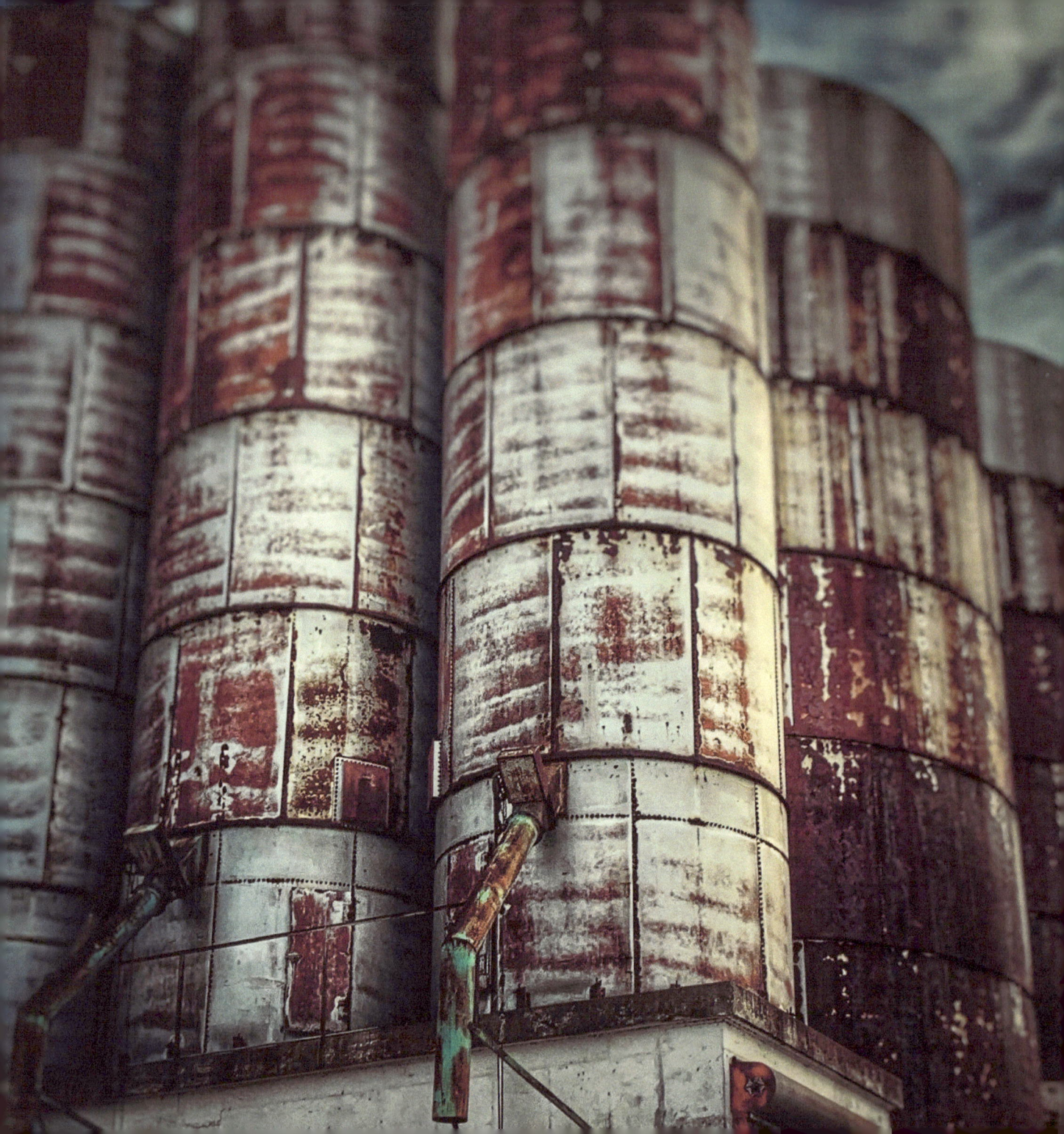

Patina

Youthful skin is a cheater
Plays in the light
with bold smoothness
and plump disregard
for sunscreen and curfew
Me?
I'm all about the patina
My surfaces and layers
oxidized by the sun
Seasons of rolling in rays
Am I envious of
your sweet skin?
Maybe
Probably
Yes
But, in these lines
lives a wisdom only
a grown ass woman
can claim

What Do the Trees Say

My heart begged me to stop
and listen to the trees
to notice the Monarch's milkweeds
and find wild indigo seed pods
skipping in the prairie's breeze

What do the twisty old oaks say?
Of generations they have witnessed
Decisions, both foolish and wise
made beneath their forked leaf canopy
What would they say about mine?

Do the willows really weep?
Wearing hearts on their lacy sleeves
Lamenting for loss and time lost
Bending and swaying with storms
Staying grounded despite the cost

And, what of my sycamore?
The big, little lady I've christened Rain
I feel her comfort, her embrace
her roots and wings fill my spirit
make me grateful and whole again

Ritual

In quiet ritual
I find reverence
Read and write
with sunrise rays
Fill the bird feeders
Being mindful of
fallen seeds and berries
Beckoning future cardinals
Nuthatches and titmouse
Hugging my tree
Thanking angels for presence
Soaking in Rain's essence
Her massive leaves a blanket
for wildflowers yet to come
In these moments
I search for self-worth
Poke around inside my rib cage
at a tattered, sulking heart
Rhythm and the blood
pulses through my body
I move onto the next
part of the day
Realizing that my worth
belongs to me and
No one else can take it away

Today, I Sit Grateful

Today, I sit grateful
My toes dangled from a rock
In one of God's rivers
My soul serene, softened
singing songs written with
lyrics of tenderness and joy
My heart paying homage
to each person who has
loved and not loved me
For places I have been
and those I will never see
For adventures I have chosen
and those I never will
Aware of our small part
in this wild and precious world
Full of grace for me
and my many faults
Grateful for days I've been lost
and for finding the way through
For the miles on my own
and those I have spent with you

Carpe Diem

Sunshine tickles eyelids
Licks the face
Don't stay asleep!
Toes peek, arms stretch
Body bursts, boisterous
Begs
B-e-c-k-o-n-s

Wake up! Wake up!
You have all of this
and all of that
And you're here
And alive!
Electric
Vibrating
Screwing up all over the place
But with laughter
and singing cells
Exploding heart
And a comforting knowing

Life isn't always serious
And a poet shouldn't be
Terminally somber
With words come weight
and responsibility
Power
Magic
Manifestation

What is your wish?
Make it
What is your jump?
Take it
Your smile?
Don't fake it
Let it caress your lips
Play at your eyes
Feel it in your chest
Launch your joy into the skies

And breathe
You've got to breathe!
Oxygen is lifeblood
Hydrogen is nectar
Gaseous miracles
Fills spaces
Cures ills
Gifts longevity
Better than pills
Carpe Diem!
Says Keating
Our span is wild and precious
And messy like finger paints
Get outta bed, you doer
Be the shaker you are, you mover
Grab your joy, love maker
Jump at the chance, risk taker
Do some work
And then some play
This life is yours
Seize the day!

In Pursuit of Goldilocks

You're not enough
—and still too much
Lead with authority
—and a woman's touch

Don't smile too big
—But don't be a bitch
Cover up your insides
—Hide your witch

The hemline of your skirt
—not too short or too long
And your hair all wispy like that
—is unprofessional and wrong

Don't be too skinny
—and GOD, don't be fat
Toot your own horn
—but not loud like that

Be nice to the guys
—they decide if you move ahead
Make friends with the wives
—Keep them all out of your bed

Run the miles
—move with the hustle
stay a little soft
—but build the muscle

Sigh, where is my porridge?
—I'm too cold and then too hot
I am who I am, Popeye says
—Not a marionette robot

Lessons in Barbed Wire

As I ran, I noticed ropes of barbed wire
held taut by iron and limestone monuments
Gravel crunched under my feet and I was
swept back to my grandpa's pastures
dotted with prairie dog mounds
Blooming with Mexican hats and thistle
He showed me the sheep mama
lodged and dying between two levels of fence
He told me that she was too stupid to back out
and too scared and paralyzed to move forward
She could have freed herself, but instead she
stayed frozen until the end of her life
Here I am, 45 years later
understanding the irony and metaphor
and grateful for Grandpa's quiet lesson
My feet pound the ground
My lungs fill with air and lead me forward
as my heart lifts out of its barbed wire cage

Soft Sadness

Inside of me lives a soft sadness
and I'm okay that it's there
Like downy milkweed in the sun
or the feather-filled pillows on the bed
Melancholy is like my pointer's loyal face
Constant companion sleeping at my feet
Most days the sorrow sits quietly, watching
or maybe follows me around the house
Puppy dog eyes hopeful for a treat
And other days, it demands my attention
Barks at me and growls; shows its teeth
Demanding I give it attention; a name
Rolls over until I acknowledge her presence
Begging me to scratch her underbelly
until she falls asleep

Flipped Switch Float Trip

I'm envious of people
whose default is joy
Of face-value thinkers
And non-pontificators
I am a thinker
A messer-insider of
brains and feeler
of all the things

Turn off the cortex, Woman!
Find some ground
Climb a tree
Sink into the water
And Girl, just be

Sunset on the lake
with friends and a paddle
Settle into the wake and
White-flag the battle

Turn over control, Honey
It's an apparition anyway
Breathe into the shore
Melt your muscles into the task

I am so lucky
Honored, blessed
I get to be here
In this moment
The pause between the
Inhale and exhale

I'm a Starseed searching for home
Finding it in Earth's eddies and pools
and old-soul eyes
Even as this orb
Spins and hurls itself
Around the sun
I know, sense, feel
that chaos is impermanent

The water invites me
—beckons me
to flip the switch off the melancholy
And remember
My default is joy

Learning How to Sleep Again

Instead of bedtime blue light
I find fireflies and cedars
Under a gibbous waxing moon
I am in natural repose
Rhythm in tune with the hum
of butterflies and bees
My limbs find the ground
melt into the forest floor
like roots burrowing
reaching for middle earth
The north breeze becomes my breath
as the day's syncopation slows
My sleepy eyes stay quiet and closed

A River Runs Through Me

Trying to grasp the Heraclitus quote
I understand that the river changes
The icy mountain water moves
amoeba and fishy bodies
up and down stream

Never to return to the same place
Living then dying and then living again
Birthed forth from the carbon ions etched
into the craggy bottom; rock and stone and slate

In forty years, have I changed?
My bone cells regenerate
Along with my blood
But have I shifted?
Am I adapting?
Or swirling in the current?
My being stays centered; stubborn
I've plotted the course and stand firm
Perhaps that's my river's magic
I abide; am scrupulous in each
toe dip I take, even when it
would take much less effort to
give in and let the water's undercurrent
sweep me up downstream and carry me away

Sleeping in an Astral Bed

Last night I laid on the deck
With a pillow, under the starry sky
The tree frogs rocked me to sleep
While the owls cooed their lullaby
In my sadness there was hope
And, maybe even a little joy
At least we shared the same moon

And though my back hurts
And my eyes are wet, teary
The quail bobwhite their greetings
And my heart is no longer weary
The cardinals sing; coaxing me awake
Quoting D.H. Lawrence with their calls
Reminding me I'm a wild thing, too

Windswept

Crazy how the wind didn't bother me
It kissed me, and I kissed it right back
Standing atop the world;
Cooper's hawk envious of our view
I ditched the heavy coat and gloves
so I could full body experience
windswept passion; the prairie's arms
    around mine
The tightest, most timeless hug I'd
    ever had
The feeling of being completely alive
even in my terminal, human
    mortality
Soaking it in, feeling it in my bones,
    breathing it into my heart
Driving home and wishing I could do
    it all over again

Forest Bath

This ritual feels right
The seasonal slow
There are no candles
No wine, no salts, no bubbles
Only the wind swirling
Tying up my hair
in twigs and sunlight
Plunging my toes into the ground
Up to my eyeballs in leaves
My body swathed in amber and rust
As I sink into the woods, I trust
That I will find a forest bath
drawn and waiting just for me

Tomatoes

Seeds
Settled into February's
soil blanket
Waiting pregnant under
the surface
and attentive eye
of the sun

Tomatoes
I can eat
like an apple
Nightshade
Bella Donna's sister
without the poison
or diva attitude

Workhorse
Salsa dancer
on the side
Canning
Peeling and processing
kitchen disco
Whirl of apron strings

Melancholy
when it's September
a whisky wine smell
Pull up the roots
and daydream
about next year's
summer harvest

Liminal Autumn

Waxing crescent
Yin's balance to the
world's perpetual yang
Time to hibernate
Rest and manifest
Ease from sun-filled days
into longer evenings
Frost lines in the morning
Patches of blue in between
swaths of burnt orange and cerise
Sleepy sprouts under the surface
Persephone's six seeds
of Hade's pomegranate
Lingering in liminal space
The pause between breath
Autumn's breeze in my face

Autumnal Equinox - A Venerable Checklist

Weave a crown of rosehips with marigolds
add to that, amber yarrow and clary sage
Forage the ground's final turnips and potatoes
Craft apples into pies and mulled cider
Share a song with the blackbirds and cicadas
where we serenade our generous Mother Earth
With gratitude, send praise for her abundance
A cornucopia draped in a sunflower garland
Ornate with acorns, maple leaves and hyssop

The sun's rays permeate my earthbound shell
as I scratch words onto paper and ask,
What will I do next with my garden?
How may I share my gifts with others?
Do my children feel my love in their separate lives?
And what of balance? Of death? Of rebirth?
For these, there are no clear answers
Only a commitment to do my best
In solemn silence and contemplation
I gather the garden's summer remnants
and prepare the ground for winter's snowy rest

Solstice March (in December)

Feeling settled into the place
where the dark meets the light
The night is long
and the day, shortened
Frost lines on the grass
Juniper berries crushed
and splattered in my hands
Saturn dances with Jupiter
And my heart stays fixed
in this moment without regard
for past issues or future worries
This place my beginning
My next step in the march
toward presence and self-compassion
Grace for others and for self
Where I let the hurts and rejection
fall away and nestle into the leaves
And wrap myself inside a patchwork quilt
close to people who are there for me
despite me being too much me

Reconnection

Come to the center of a quiet spot
Breathe into your spaces
Root - limbs - belly - heart
Reach inside for inner knowing
Be kind to yourself as you turn
to the dog-eared pages;
Bookmarked experience and time
What questions are surfacing?
Reconnect with your intuition
What you seek is already looking for you
You will find your answers living there

Sunflower

Pluck my buttery petals;
Sprinkle them atop
your sensuous, silken bath

Kiss my smile;
Lace my lips inside
your sunny, exuberant laugh

Lean into me;
Lay heavy against
my languorous length

Trace your fingers;
Anchored at the stem
harness my will, my strength

With our backs
against the wind
Our faces to the sun
Let's lift our hearts to
hopeful, joy-filled days
Toe-dip in the prairie's glow
Feel the warmth, embrace the fun

Moon in Passing

Today the moon passed
Between the Earth and Sun
A celestial invitation; a call
to reclaim personal power
My heart shifted and my eyes
Found the radiance pop
from the behind the clouds
I'd like to say that suddenly
clarity sat on my lap and slapped
me in the face, but no,
never is that the case
Still; always there is a hope
that lucidity will replace lunacy
Until then, I'll wave to the moon in passing
And she'll tip her umbral beams to me

Hanging Curve Ball of Space

Lying on my back, making wishes on the moon
Front row seats on this third rock planet
Contemplating light years, quantum physics
Laughing out loud, because I know nothing

Humankind is immersed in a giant snail shell
Fibonacci's sunflower swirl
Our atoms collide in bent, curved
Undulating, hologram images
Like a pretzeled yogi, the sun bends around itself
As our existence tick tocks around its rays

We are spec of matter in the Creator's playpen
Unique, beautiful, but insignificant
under a cosmic canopy of sky

Oh, Einstein!
I want to shimmy with you under the stars
Lasso their luminescent spurs
Peek under Cassiopeia's skirt
Dip the snipped hem of my lacy dress
into the stardust bunnies of the Milky Way

The galaxy is my soul sister
my perpetual partner in a planetary dance
Together, our insides explode, collapse, and ripple
sway like the waves on the surface of the sea
The movement is sublime
Dip, dive, and swerve to
Fight gravity
And relativity, stop time

In the Pecan Orchard

I want to read to you this morning
Let you ease into this early day
Your head on my lap; eyes half-closed
Lashes fanned, breath steady
With your lengthened, nourishing exhales
I'd wax words about growing pecans
and how trees in an orchard
naturally take care of each other
Sharing water and resources
Roots crawling to earth's center
As their limbs reach for sun
Discuss with you how when one tree fruits
all of the trees in the orchard will fruit, too
The meat of their labor feeding forest four-leggeds
and how your sweet, wonderful soul feeds mine

Unsupervised

Freedom
It's relative
Depending if it's
an eagle eye's view
or Eagle's lyrics
Don and Glenn
In a year where
freedom was my goal
I am cagey
4 1/2 hours
of unsupervised time
was more than total
moments combined
in the 333 days prior
It's not lost on me
I'm not alone
I'm happy to figure it out
Hold your hand while we do
I've created my own prison
Like the chains to my desk
and straps around my ankles
I am the one holding the keys

Sinusoidal Curves

You wrote an equation
Graphed the sunrise
and sunset for a year
And, I wondered
What does that look like?
Did you capture the essence
in hyperbolic lines and graph points?
Or did you sketch and pencil shade
sides of the moon and sunbeams
in a rise to the top of the paper
and back down again?
You told me it was an X-Y graph
with two sinusoidal curves
And all I could do was smile

You route the orbit of planets
Understand azimuth and trajectory
And, I wonder
What would it feel like?
To lie on our backs
Your shoulder next to mine
To have intimate knowledge
of those minute balls of gas
Glitter on a black velvet blanket
Spread across the night's sky
Millions and billions of light years
A curtain call encore showing
A Sin (sign) just for us

Scent of Soon It'll be Autumn

The scent of soon it'll be Autumn
ambled through the window
and moseyed into my nose
My mind went to steamy mugs
Cinnamon rolls teetering atop
brown brick bowls of hearty chilly
And suddenly, I'm wrapped inside
the cashmere blanket of your arms
My face tucked, tickling the
inviting crook of your neck
Your nose nuzzled into
the crown of my head
My fingers wandering, roaming
Coaxing, inviting you to stay in bed

Following the Azimuth

Time comes at you fast
When it moves so slow
We know not the day
Try to plot our path
With azimuth and vector
A personal pilgrimage
To our North Star
A Ram Das nudge
to grab your hand
Walk you home
The bough of a hickory
A maple or an oak
Branches for birds
Their nests a haven
for life's next cycle
Roots for fungi and bugs
Sunlight on the crown
The trip ends here
Until we are reborn
When our ashes
find the ground

Lay my Limbs

Let me lay my limbs next to yours
Allow our fingers to find the earth
Scratch together a blanket of leaves
Your broken pieces lock into mine
Swirling inside the sanctity of moonlight
Feel our hearts sync inside the breeze
Home bound; under the cover of walnut trees

The View

I see you perched on the dock
Rainbow over your shoulder
Knowing more than what
most people ever will
It's the view, ya'know?
But, you never know
what you don't know
Until you do
All you want
is one last look
one more time
another moment
to see the view

About the Author

Michelle Terry is a dreamer, storm chaser, and forest bather with ~~mountain climbing~~ skinny dipping still on her bucket list. Michelle also suffers from shiny object syndrome with a penchant for getting lost in strange places.

In *Little Women*, after Amy burned Jo's manuscript, Michelle wrote several burn-worthy stories and poetry of her own. She was nine. After multiple rejections from *Reader's Digest* and *Good Housekeeping*, she chose a reasonable degree in dietetics and nutrition.

Writing as Mama Mick, she dabbled in humor blogging until she discovered she wasn't funny. She wrote for several local and regional magazines and made the editors bonkers with her non-journalistic voice and personal approach to human interest stories. Since she was a girl, photographing storm clouds from a farm in northcentral Kansas, Michelle finally purchased a real camera and donned a poet's pen after her last child left the nest. Her poetry is non-traditional and crafted for an audience who wants to read without getting a headache. Her photography will never be technically sound, but it's authentic and tells a story all its own.

The author has published in *Kansas! Magazine*, *Topeka Magazine*, and *NASCAR Illustrated*. *Hidden Hikes*, her most recent contribution to *Kansas! Magazine* partially inspired the book you are holding in your hands. This book is the first of three in a series.

During the day, Michelle works as a clinical dietitian and account manager in Alzheimer's disease. When she is not working, running, doing yoga, or wrangling a family, you'll find her in the garden wearing mud boots and a sundress pulling weeds.

You can find her photos on Instagram @mamamickterry and her photo-inspired poetry @hiding_owl_diaries and at www.michellerterry.com.

Acknowledgments

To Kansas: You were my first love. Your sunsets, sunrises, and open prairies will always hold a place in my stormy heart.

To the University of Arkansas senior marketing students: Phillip Rouse, Hannah Bradle, and Carly Mason. I loved and appreciated the joy you infused into this book. I know you'll do great things. Go Razorbacks!

To David Braughler and Craig Ramsdell of Braughler Books: I knew we'd work together when I met David at the Erma Bombeck convention over 5 years ago. Thank you so much for taking my snippets of writing and dropbox photo files and creating something beyond my wildest dreams. You have been a joy to work with, and I cannot wait to do it again. Are you game??

To my favorite photographers: Jonathan, Sissy, Sheena, Maria, Susan, Erica, Rachel, Pat, Zach, Karla, Laura, Diane, Cody, Jeff, Bri, and Ray. An extra shout to Ray for keeping me honest and calling bullshit as needed. Which apparently, was a lot.

To Christy and Jenny: You introduced me to the poetry of Mary Oliver, Emily Dickinson, and Dorianne Laux. You encouraged me to write without filters, and that blood, wrinkles, and scars could still be beautiful. You were the first poets I ever read, and I'm forever grateful for the Lovely Fire years.

To Cody: Thank you for imprinting your Libra OCD tendencies in these edits to fix my mostly crooked, often poorly exposed photography. And thank you for shooting the Windswept center spread and biography photo — you know how I dislike being on the wrong end of the camera. I appreciate the childlike innocence and joy you have infused into these pages. I couldn't have done it without you.

To the friends I've not yet met: You know who you are! Thank you for reading my Instagram poems and liking my photos. Your encouragement and engagement mean the world.

To Mom (Marguerite), Dad (Bob), and both grandmas (Leona and Nora): You taught me how to notice nature's beauty with a grateful and discerning eye. I learned how to build fences, pick weeds and strawberries right out of the garden. I love you soo much!

To Ron and Marie: You didn't sign up for a daughter like me. Thank you for accepting me then and now. I love you both very much.

To Tanna, Dane, and Scott: Thank you for decades of laughter, tears, and shenanigans. You've had to practice patience so many times when I asked to jump out of the car to snap a photo or missed dinner because the sunset kept me away. Not every year was easy, but they were all blessed in some way. Thank you for your compassion, understanding, and unconditional love of my gypsy heart.

To the reader: Yes. You. Thank you for being here.

www.ingramcontent.com/pod-product-compliance
Lightning Source LLC
Chambersburg PA
CBHW040356190426
43201CB00040B/42